DOG Coloring Book For Kids

This Coloring book Belongs to:

....

....

Try Your Coloring Pencil Before Coloring

Try Your Coloring Pencil Before Coloring

Try Your Coloring Pencil

Before Coloring

Try Your Coloring Pencil Before Coloring

Try Your Coloring Pencil Before Coloring

Try Your Coloring Pencil Before Coloring

Try Your Coloring Pencil Before Coloring

Try Your Coloring Pencil Before Coloring

Try Your Coloring Pencil
Before Coloring

Try Your Coloring Pencil Before Coloring

Try Your Coloring Pencil Before Coloring

Try Your Coloring Pencil Before Coloring

Try Your Coloring Pencil Before Coloring

Try Your Coloring Pencil Before Coloring

Try Your Coloring Pencil Before Coloring

Try Your Coloring Pencil
Before Coloring

Try Your Coloring Pencil Before Coloring

Try Your Coloring Pencil

Before Coloring

Try Your Coloring Pencil Before Coloring

Try Your Coloring Pencil Before Coloring

Try Your Coloring Pencil Before Coloring

Try Your Coloring Pencil Before Coloring

Try Your Coloring Pencil Before Coloring

Try Your Coloring Pencil Before Coloring

Try Your Coloring Pencil Before Coloring

Try Your Coloring Pencil
Before Coloring

Try Your Coloring Pencil Before Coloring

Try Your Coloring Pencil Before Coloring

DOG

Try Your Coloring Pencil

Before Coloring

Try Your Coloring Pencil Before Coloring

Try Your Coloring Pencil Before Coloring

Try Your Coloring Pencil Before Coloring

Try Your Coloring Pencil Before Coloring